# THE LITTLE BOOK OF
# GARDENING TIPS

## A practical guide to Gardening

# THE LITTLE BOOK OF
# GARDENING TIPS
## A practical guide to Gardening

This edition first published in the UK in 2008
By Green Umbrella Publishing

© Green Umbrella Publishing 2008

**www.gupublishing.co.uk**

Publishers Jules Gammond & Vanessa Gardner

Printed and bound in China

ISBN 978-1-906229-61-0

# THE LITTLE BOOK OF
# GARDENING TIPS
## A practical guide to Gardening

**Written by David Curnock**

# 1

Anyone can grow plants – even without a garden: plants can be grown in a window box, flower pot, growing bag or, in water, using a simple hydroponics kit. From the smallest pot plant, to the largest garden or allotment, the achievement of growing a single living plant, or reaping a harvest of vegetables, is the same, regardless of scale. Many children have experienced the joy of growing cress on a damp flannel or blotting paper, this being the simplest form of hydroponics; if a child can succeed, it should not be difficult for anybody to achieve some success, when growing plants. Whether spending a few pence or a fortune, a little forethought can make a great difference to the final outcome. Just have a go!

# 2

Decide on what you want to achieve with your available gardening resources, whether they be plant pots, window boxes, patio tubs, flower beds, or a vegetable patch. Each of these can yield the reward of some form of crop, be it the simple joy of seeing a flower in bloom, the picking of fresh produce for the dining table, or the economic benefit from growing large quantities of staple vegetables. Most plants need light, warmth, water, and space to grow; some also need a means of support – bear these simple requirements in mind, then decide what you intend to grow.

# 3

On a fairly dry but not sun-baked day, take a handful of soil and squeeze it between your fingers. The ideal soil should have a dark, crumb-like texture, and is known as loam. If the soil separates into sandy grains, it is said to be sandy, and will generally be free draining, and will require frequent watering. Pale, light soil may be chalky, and will also drain freely. On the other hand, dark, rich brown soil may be peaty, and could easily become waterlogged. Clay soil is readily apparent as it has a smoother, 'shiny' appearance, and will prevent proper drainage. Choose plants according to the soil texture and pH characteristics of your soil.

# 4

Some plants will only thrive on a particular type of soil, either acidic or alkaline. Planting in the wrong type of soil will often result in failure, and can be expensive. Before planting, it is advisable to test for the acidity level, commonly referred to as the pH (potential of Hydrogen), present in the soil. This can be achieved by purchasing a soil testing kit from a garden supplies centre, or plant nursery. Take samples from the soil using a hand trowel at 2m (6ft) intervals and at a depth of 15cm (6in). Do not handle the soil directly as this can affect the result. Mix all of the samples together in a dry, clean bucket or plastic bag, then take a small amount for use with the testing kit. Follow the instructions on the kit to determine the acidity level in the soil sample.

# 5

Once the soil pH is known, this can be used to help in deciding on the choice of plants to be grown. Soil that is too alkaline can be adjusted by adding leaf mould or peat-based compost; acidic soil can be adjusted by adding garden lime. Plants that prefer a particular soil type may be grown in a soil that would otherwise be considered unsuitable by locally dressing the soil, both before planting and regularly, thereafter. Rhododendrons, azaleas, and pieris shrubs all can each be planted in a hole that has been prepared with the addition of a special, ericaceous compost that is suitable for acid-loving plants, and the soil regularly top-dressed with this same compost to maintain the pH level.

# 6

Some plants will tolerate soil that is either acidic or alkaline: the Hydrangea Macrophylla blossoms in pink or blue, depending on the soil pH. In acidic soils, the flowers are blue; in alkaline soils, the flowers are pink. Soil of any type can always be adjusted, and its structure and texture improved: back-breaking, clay soil can be lightened by first digging over to expose the heavy clumps to winter frost, then adding organic drainage material, such as horse stable manure, containing straw. On clay soils, it is essential to regularly incorporate organic material to assist with drainage. The addition of garden lime will also help to build up a 'crumb' structure within the soil.

# 7

Poor drainage can kill plants just as easily as can the lack of water; stagnant water that lies in poorly drained soil can deprive the roots of air, and may rot some root fibres. Excessive drainage, caused by sandy soil, will result in the need for frequent watering. In excessively sandy soil conditions, the use of copious quantities of humus material, from the stable or farmyard, will assist in retaining some of the moisture, as well as introducing nutrients. Find out what type of soil structure you have in your garden, and its pH level, and then purchase plants accordingly.

# 8

While this dry storage technique is not suitable for every type of plant seed, it can be used for most. Flower heads that have set seed, and started to dry, can be put into a paper bag to catch the seed as it is released. Place seed into an envelope labelled with the plant variety and, most importantly, the planting and flowering season details. It is always a good thing to retain the original seed packet for information on planting. Fruit and vegetable seeds can be saved in a similar manner but must first be cleaned, and dried, before storing. Place seed packets or envelopes in an airtight jar or container containing a desiccant, and store in a cool, dark and dry place, at a temperature between 0-5°C (32-41°F). The domestic refrigerator is ideal for this purpose.

# 9

Every garden produces waste matter. Lawn grass cuttings, hedge trimmings, or even waste vegetable tops and other kitchen trimmings (except meats), can all be put to productive use in the gardener's compost heap or bin. Small compost bins can be purchased 'ready to go' or in a self-assembly pack: larger amounts of waste garden products can be composted in a custom-built container that need cost very little. Some fence posts with chicken wire wrapped around them can be very effective, but remember to leave the bottom front section easily detachable to enable your (almost) free compost to be removed. Compost requires warmth, so it may need to be covered with some old carpet or similar. Make alternate layers of fine clippings of grass and straw, leaves, or shredded twigs to ensure good drainage. Do not put perennial weeds, or seeded weeds, in the bin.

# 10

Plant your spring flowering bulbs from September onwards. Choose bulbs carefully to ensure that they are healthy; select bulbs as you would choose onions in a vegetable shop, and reject any that are soft, damaged or discoloured. Generally, plant bulbs at a depth of around 2-3 times their length; in frost prone areas this should be increased to around 4-5 times their length. Additional protection can be provided with a mulch of bark chippings. Some gardeners prefer to place their bulbs in a cool refrigerator for a few days before planting; this is said to be beneficial, and ensures that the bulb starts to grow when placed in the, comparatively, warmer soil, resulting in earlier flowering.

# 11

Some types of plants are too tender to be planted outdoors until all chance of frost has passed; in some areas, this can be late in May, or early June. In order to maximise their growing season, seeds can be sown indoors in March, or early April. This is done by sowing seed in shallow seed trays, or in plant pots, using seed compost. Do not use garden soil as this may contain weeds or parasites that may harm the seed or seedlings; better results will be obtained using the correct compost.

# 12

Ideally, seed should be sown in a peat-based compost that has been sterilised, and fortified with nutrients. Most proprietary seed composts meet these requirements. Level the compost in the seed tray using a straight-edge: do not compact the soil. Water the compost, but do not soak, using a hand sprayer or fine rose watering can. Sow seed thinly, then cover with a thin layer of compost. Generally, small seeds are left uncovered, so follow the directions on the packet. Place the finished tray in a warm place, between 60ºF and 70ºF (15.5-21ºC) is ideal. Cover with glass, and place a sheet of brown paper on top. Dry the glass, and turn it every day; this prevents condensation from making the compost too wet. When seedlings appear, remove the paper, prop up the glass to allow air to circulate, and place the tray in good daylight, turning regularly to prevent uneven growth.

# 13

Seedlings should be pricked out into seed trays or plant pots that contain a potting compost. Prick out when two pairs of leaves have formed. Handle seedlings by their leaves, not by their roots or stems, as this could cause damage. Space out at 1½-inch (40mm) intervals and place in the shade for a day or two. Harden off, by placing in a cool room indoors, or cold frame outdoors, for a day or two, then place outside during the daytime for several days. Leave outside at night for a week or so, ensuring no frost is forecast, before finally planting out in position.

# 14

Seeds can also be sown in small pots, indoors, in a warm place between 60-70ºF (15.5-21ºC). The pots should be covered with a clear polythene bag, secured with a rubber band or plant tie. When the seedlings appear, remove the bag, place the pot on a light window sill, away from direct sunlight. Turn the pot regularly to avoid lopsided growth, and remember to keep the compost moist, but not wet. Prick out seedlings, and harden off, as before.

# 15

Growing bags can be used almost anywhere, and are an ideal way to grow tomatoes, aubergines, chillies and cucumbers, on sunny patios and balconies, as well as in the greenhouse. Don't forget to label with the plant variety and, if a novice gardener, add care instructions about pinching out shoots, etc. If the growing bag is on an upper floor balcony, be a good neighbour, and try to prevent water from draining onto the downstairs properties.

# 16

Before planting a growing bag, loosen the compost in the bag by first shaking it, and then kneading, to break up any lumps. After first piercing the bottom of the bag for drainage, shape the bag into an even, slightly humped form, and ensure the compost is evenly distributed. Cut out the marked areas on the bag for planting larger plants, such as tomatoes and courgettes – or cut out a long rectangle for rows of smaller plants. Scoop out sufficient compost to accept the root ball of the plant, place the plant in the hole with the top of the root ball just below the top surface of the compost, then infill compost around the plant. Lightly firm in the plant, using finger tips or a small stick of wood, then water well.

# 17

If designing from scratch, or making major changes to the layout of an existing garden, remember a few simple guidelines. Make all cultivated areas easily accessible. It is a good idea to plan for access by wheelchair or walking-frame users; you may not always be fully fit and active, so it is sensible to plan for any eventuality! Where possible, sheds and greenhouses should also be easily accessible, preferably reached from hardened pathways.

# 18

A patio can provide a means of growing throughout the year, even in winter, when the soil in the garden is unfit for working. Container plants, or small beds set into the patio area, can provide a year-round display of colour. Containers also give the gardener an opportunity to move them around to create a new aspect. A grey winter day can be brightened by planting colourful foliage plants in containers, which can then be placed where they can be seen through a patio door or window.

# 19

When planting fruit trees, take into account the potential height of the plant for pruning and gathering of crops. Many varieties of fruit may be grown in even the smallest garden so, think vertical! Use a convenient south-facing wall or fence, against which can be planted fruit trees that can be both productive, as well as softening the harsh appearance of the structure. In more southerly areas, some quite exotic fruits may be grown including peach, grapes, and other Mediterranean varieties.

# 20

Espalier and cordon-trained fruit trees can provide good crops within a height of around 1.5 to 2 metres from the ground. Most of these require some support, in the form of wires or trellis, against which they may be tied-in. This will make things easier when it comes to pruning as the leader shoots and fruiting 'spurs' will be more readily apparent. Similarly, small bush fruit trees, such as gooseberry, red- and blackcurrant and the like, will be simpler to maintain, and their fruit gathered more easily, if they can be reached from a pathway. This will also help to prevent soil compaction around plants by restricting the need to tread on the surrounding soil.

# 21

Try companion planting to deter pests or as an aid to pollination. Plant companions at the same time to get the best results. French marigolds planted in between tomato plants will deter aphids. Similarly, garlic planted near roses will also keep aphids at bay. Apart from being a useful herb in the kitchen, dill will attract aphid-eating hoverflies into the garden. Carrots and leeks, when planted near each other, mutually deter each other's pests. Nasturtiums planted near cabbages help to protect the cabbages from caterpillars, and give a splash of colour when they flower.

# 22

Regularly dead-head flowering plants to prolong their season. When flowers have been successfully pollinated, they will 'set seed'; the flowers will fade and die, and the plants will devote all their energies into seed production. Dead-heading removes the faded flower with its pollinated seed, and thus encourages the plant to produce even more flowers, in order that it may set further seeds, as nature intended. Some seed heads may be left to ripen and dry, if it is planned to retain the seed for the following season. Do not remove flowers from fruit or ornamental trees, otherwise no produce or berries will appear!

# 23

Vegetable and flower beds, and garden borders, should be planted where they can be reached easily from one or both sides, to avoid unnecessary strain when working. For the less mobile, raised beds, that can be easily tended from a wheelchair or while seated, are a great way to both take the strain out of the back muscles, as well as providing a variation in levels that could add to the eye appeal of the garden. Coupled with hard landscaping of paths and patios, these raised beds can help reduce the cultivated area of a large garden when its upkeep begins to take its toll on the weary; however, overuse of hard landscaping can make a garden take on the appearance of a car park. There is also the potential to affect both the drainage, and the wildlife, in the area.

# 24

For the novice gardener, herbs are an ideal starting point. Annuals such as basil, coriander, and marjoram, and the perennial mint, fennel and thyme, can all be grown in almost any sunny spot, either in containers, in a formal herb garden or in borders. Be warned that some varieties of mint, especially, can be invasive, and will soon begin to take over: these plants are best grown in containers to keep them under control. Woody perennials, such as rosemary and sage, can make an attractive feature, or form a division between areas of the garden, as well as being useful in the kitchen.

# 25

Always use the correct tool for the job in hand, and wear personal protection for the eyes and hands. On sunny days, protect the head and neck and wear long sleeves or, better still, sit in the shade with a cooling drink, and plan the next job to be done, until the heat of the day has passed. Gardening can be hard work – but only if you make it so!

# 26

Annual-flowering plants that particularly benefit from regular dead-heading are those most frequently grown in hanging baskets and containers. These include Petunias, Pelargoniums (Geraniums), Busy Lizzies (Impatiens), Roses, and Begonias. Bulbs may also be dead-headed, as this will allow the bulbous root to conserve energy for the next season. With the exception of the late-flowering varieties, the flowering season of many climbing plants will be extended, especially the Rose, although this often thorny plant may fight back! Wear suitable protection against thorns, and don't exceed your comfortable reach or height.

# 27

Some plants should not be dead-headed at all: included in this group are the late-flowering Clematis Clematis orientalis, Honesty Lunaria, Firethorn Pyracantha, and most ornamental grasses. Other annuals and biennials will not produce any more flowers after dead-heading, so bear this in mind. On the other hand, certain annuals may even oblige with a second flush of flowers, after being cut back to the base after the first flush has finished, a good example being the Lupin Lupinus. It is always worthwhile having a try. Dead-head with the fingers on soft, fleshy stems, or with secateurs or garden scissors on woody stems.

# 28

Vegetables need good light, water, good drainage, and protection from the wind. Endeavour to satisfy these requirements, and protect them against wildlife. Birds, especially pigeons, can be a particular problem when the young, green leaves start to appear. Take suitable precautions and use netting, or other forms of protection, against these free loaders! Fruit trees also need some form of defence against the local animal population; crows and magpies love apples, while rabbits will eat most salad crops and their favourite root vegetable, (as recommended by Bugs Bunny), the carrot.

# 29

Hedge plants can provide protection against the wind, but they also drink freely from the moisture in the soil, drying out considerable areas. Rather than plant a hedge on an exposed site, particularly in a smaller garden, consider the use of Hessian or similar material to form a windbreak, thus reducing the number of journeys to be made while carrying the gardener's friend, the watering can. Avoid planting under overhanging trees; these also take up copious amounts of water, as well as reducing the light available to the plants. These parts of the garden can be planted with varieties that prefer cooler, shady conditions.

# 30

Jobs to be done in spring: Fork over any bare soil in vegetable beds, then rake or sift soil and prepare for planting shallots and onion sets. Sow early salad and vegetable seeds and cover with cloches or a poly-tunnel. Plant potato tubers, if sufficiently sprouted, and most main crop vegetables – but leave the frost tender varieties until all likelihood of frost has passed. Plant tomatoes in unheated greenhouse or poly-tunnel. Feed soft fruit trees and bushes.

# 31

In summer: Clear out empty beds after harvesting early salad and vegetables, and replant with different main crop varieties – remember to rotate! Feed and water tomatoes, peppers, aubergines, melons and cucumbers, and remove any unwanted side shoots. Pick your well-deserved crop of strawberries, then plant any new strawberry plants. Protect existing soft fruit plants from birds – they will know when things are good to eat, long before you do! Provide protection for the greenhouse plants with either exterior 'paint-on' or, re-usable internal shading, and ventilate well. Earth up potatoes, and plant winter brassicas (cabbage, Brussels sprouts, etc).

# 32

Autumn is the time to empty, clean and disinfect the greenhouse. Don't forget to wash pots and seed trays to prevent infection of your next year's plants. Dig and manure empty flower and vegetable beds. This is a good time to plant soft fruit trees and bushes – you should be reaping your reward from any established fruit around this time. Dig up main crop potatoes, dry them in the fresh air, then store in paper sacks (do not use plastic!) in a cool, dry shed or garage. Sow winter salads under glass. Fruit trees that have dropped all their leaves can now be pruned, if necessary.

# 33

Where possible use vertical space in the garden, and grow crops of climbing vegetables, or flowers. A simple net stretched between two or more uprights can support a variety of plants, including beans, gourds, cucumbers and even melons, although these do require plenty of water. Similarly, a tepee or wigwam of bamboo canes or willow stalks, placed in a container, can be a valuable cropping source where space is limited, and can be sited almost anywhere, as long as there is good daylight, and not too much wind. Tomatoes and bell peppers can be grown in containers on any warm, sunny patio or balcony.

# 34

Productive crops, especially those with large leaves or fruits, can be very thirsty. Keep an eye on them at all times, especially in hot weather, watching for sign of wilting. Most plants will look a little 'under the weather' in adverse conditions, so carry out any watering in the evening or early morning, when there is little or no sun. Watering in the heat of the day will offer some relief to your plants, but could have an adverse effect on your water utility charge.

# 35

When watering, give everything a good soaking, not a light spray. A hole, made with a broom handle or dibber, alongside the root of the plant will ensure that water penetrates deeply enough to promote good root growth, and will not evaporate too quickly. For some plants, such as leeks, many gardeners advocate the use of a length of waste water pipe, placed vertically in the soil alongside the plant, to facilitate deep watering.

# 36

For the larger garden, or in places where it can be difficult to reach, consider the use of an irrigation system. These can be purchased in kit form and adapted to suit almost any watering situation, from borders and vegetable patch, to hanging baskets or window boxes. Various nozzles, branches, and adjustable flow regulators, help to ensure that each plant or location receives the correct amount of liquid, thus minimising waste, and also avoids the need for many trips to the water butt.

# 37

Irrigation systems offer a flexible, targeted solution to most garden and greenhouse watering situations. They can also be fitted with a programmable timer unit; this allows the watering ritual to take place at any selected hour of the day, or night, without the need for the gardener to be present, making the occasional weekend away from home a distinct possibility. Don't stay away too long, though – the weeds will soon take over!

# 38

One vital piece of garden equipment is the water butt. This can be fitted close to a rainwater downpipe and is filled, for free, in wet weather. It will provide a valuable supply of water for the garden, particularly in dry periods, when there may be a ban on the use of hose pipes and irrigation systems. Several water butts can be linked together in a daisy-chain, with the overflow from each butt feeding into the next, in sequence. Rainwater, being softer than tap water, is also less likely to leave unsightly spotting on the leaves of plants.

# 39

Weeds take water, light, and nutrients from your plants: take precautions against them. The use of mulches, including leaf mould, tree bark chippings, or black plastic sheeting, can restrict the growth of weeds between plants, and in non-planted areas of the garden. Although black plastic may not look very pretty, it is the gardener's best ally against the weed. A heavily weed-covered area of ground can be reclaimed by overlaying it with dense black plastic sheeting – even the most stubborn weeds need light, although the cover may need to be in place for some weeks for this to be successful.

# 40

Before the harsher days of winter, there is plenty to do: collect any leaves and unwanted vegetable tops for composting. Harvest and store late cropping vegetables. Brassicas can generally look after themselves, but you will need to harvest root crops before the frosts become severe. Store in a cool, dry place, as for potatoes. Dig and manure the empty beds afterwards. By now, the seed catalogues should be available, so give some thought towards the things you want to grow next year, and place your order early. If you are over-wintering tender plants in the greenhouse, check that your anti-frost heater is serviceable.

# 41

The first defence against weeds is to remove any roots found when digging over the plot. This can be laborious, and time consuming, but is worthwhile. However, the act of digging can break off small portions of the weed root, which will grow rapidly to form a new plant. It may bring to the surface those seeds from weeds that have flowered, even several years ago, to live another day. A combination of weed control measures may need to be taken, including the use of weed-killers: these should be used with extreme caution, as they may cause damage to, or even kill, other plants. Where necessary, use strictly according to the instructions provided, and store in a safe, secure place.

# 42

The tap root of the dandelion can reach over six inches (150mm) in length. Left alone, it will grow again and, if left to set seed, can produce over 5,000 new dandelion weeds. These seeds are popular with children, and are known in folklore as 'clocks', the number of times taken to blow all the seeds from the head is said to indicate the time of day. The seeds 'broadcast' themselves downwind on their downy parachutes. Always remove the root completely; a tell-tale snapping noise, when pulling or digging, will indicate the job has not been done properly. Dig it out!

# 43

Paths and driveways may be cleared, or kept free, of weeds by the use of chemicals that have been specially developed for the purpose. An alternative to the use of chemicals is the flame gun. This acts in a manner similar to that of a blow torch, and is particularly suitable for killing surface weeds and their seeds, that may lie on, or just below, the surface of earthen or aggregate pathways.

# 44

Lawns are a very different problem; individual weeds can be 'spot' treated with a herbicidal pen, or lawn sand. Larger areas are usually dealt with by using an overall treatment that contains a herbicide against the weeds, as well as a fertiliser that will promote growth and 'greening' of the lawn grass. This type of treatment can be found in either a granular or liquid form, and is applied during the growing season, usually May to September.

# 45

Garden plants do not live on water alone. In ideal soil conditions they receive their nutrients from the soil but, as the soil becomes spent, it is necessary to replenish the plant's larder. This is not as straightforward as it may seem; just spreading granulated or liquid fertiliser on the soil is simply not good enough. Different types of plants require a particular type of nutrient for good results: generally, leafy crops require the addition of nitrogen-based fertilisers, while fruiting plants need plenty of potash; tomato plants do best with a magnesium supplement. It should be remembered that you will eventually eat the fruit and vegetables, so go easy with the chemicals!

# 46

For those who have a dislike for chemical additives, there is always the organic option. Many gardeners shun the use of potentially harmful substances in the soil and, although there may be a slight reduction in yield, or some increase in damage from pests, prefer to use only organic controls and additives. Biological materials, such as well-rotted farmyard manure, garden or spent mushroom compost, all help to improve the fertility of the soil and its structure, and have served gardeners well for many years, prior to the advent of chemical products.

# 47

Organic plant foods will provide additional nutrients to satisfy particular requirements. bonemeal, hoof and horn, wood ash, and fish, blood and bone are all high in nitrogen and phosphates. Seaweed stimulates plant roots, while garden lime increases calcium. Most of these organics are supplied as powder or granules, suitable for hand dressing the soil. Concentrated animal manure, known as urea, can be applied either as a liquid, or in granular form, and is one of the most natural, and fast-acting, means of increasing the nitrogen in soil.

# 48

Pest control can also be achieved by largely natural means, if you encourage certain predators into the garden. Instead of using slug pellets, there are biological substitutes: products containing a natural parasite of slugs, known as nematodes (Phasmarhabditis Hermaphrodita), work against slugs both above and below the surface of the soil. Usually supplied in powder form, this type of product is diluted with water for use, and is child and pet safe; it is also harmless to birds and hedgehogs who may dine on the slugs afterwards. A treatment can last for up to six weeks, and the product remains active during wet weather.

# 49

Copper contains a small positive charge that repels slugs, and forms a barrier across which they will not cross. The use of copper slug rings around the slugs' favourite plants is very effective, and these rings can be slotted together to protect larger, or awkwardly-shaped plant structures. Plants in pots can be similarly protected by placing self-adhesive copper tape around them, just below the rim. Copper snail tape has a serrated edge that snails find impassable as they climb the plant pot: snail tape is also effective against slugs, so it makes good sense to purchase this dual-purpose version.

# 50

The adult vine weevil feeds on plant foliage during the summer and autumn, leaving U-shaped cut-outs from the edge of the leaf. Up to 1cm long, brownish-black in colour, with drab yellow spots on its back, it is quick moving, nocturnal, and can be difficult to spot. Vine weevils are particularly fond of Rhododendrons, Camellias and Azaleas, as well as enjoying a wide range of herbaceous plants. They cause damage only to the edge of the leaf; although this can be unsightly, it does not seriously harm the plant, unless weevils are present in large numbers.

# 51

Plants that appear to wilt, even though the soil or compost is moist, are probably under attack by the larvae of the vine weevil. In the worst scenario, usually in dryer soils and composts, the plant will topple as its root system is destroyed. The adult vine weevils lay their eggs in the root balls of plants, which then hatch into grubs that feed on the roots, before over-wintering. On emerging as adult weevils, they repeat the cycle. Vine weevil larvae are cream-white in colour, and about 1cm in length. Treatment against these pests should be carried out in spring and autumn, using a nematode biological treatment such as Nemasys®.

# 52

Aphids are among the most troublesome pests, both in the greenhouse and outdoors, attacking a wide range of plants. They are usually either green or black, hence their common names greenfly and blackfly. Aphids feed by sucking the sap from the tender new shoots of the plant; this stunts the growth, and causes distortion of the growing point. The aphid absorbs large quantities of plant sap in order to obtain enough protein; the sap contains sugar that the aphid excretes as honeydew. This bubble-like excretion is probably the first indication of their presence, unless the gardener is particularly watchful.

# 53

Aphids also carry virus diseases which may result in long term harm to the plants. Spray affected areas with a soap solution, or remove aphids by hand. A more elegant solution – no pun intended! – is to place adult ladybirds, or the larvae of the lacewing, on the plants affected. There are commercial suppliers of these natural predators (available when in season): each lacewing larvae will eat several hundred aphids before becoming an adult: they will also control red spider mite, and whitefly. Adult ladybirds (adalia bipunctata) are useful in both the garden and greenhouse. The introduction of this aphid-loving predator will reward you by keeping the pests under control, while also being good to look at.

# 54

Leatherjackets are the larval stage of the crane fly, commonly known as 'daddy long legs', and can have a devastating effect on a lawn. The larvae are about 2.5cm (1 inch) long, greyish-black in colour, legless, and with no distinct head. The crane fly lays its eggs in late August, and they hatch within 2 weeks. The young start to feed immediately, and will continue to feed throughout the winter, ready to feast on the fresh growth of grass roots the following spring. Their natural enemy, apart from birds, is a parasitic nematode called Steinernema Feltiae, which kills leatherjackets but is harmless to children, wildlife and pets. This parasite should be introduced in September or October, while the soil temperature is still fairly warm, above 10ºC (50ºF).

# 55

Ants can be another major headache for gardeners, in lawns, cultivated beds, and borders. The application of boiling water will usually eradicate them from cracks in pathways and driveways but, if used on lawns and around plants, can cause more damage than the pests themselves. Again, nematodes are an effective remedy, as is the use of Diatomaceous Earth, a fine powder obtained from fossilised remains of an algae, and is supplied in a puffer-dispenser for ease of use.

# 56

Blackspot and mildew on roses and fruit trees, especially apples, pears, and cane fruits, can be treated with a sulphur-based spray. This treatment should be carried out during the growing season, and must be applied to both sides of the leaves; a pressure sprayer fitted with a lance is ideal for this purpose. Do not spray fruit trees that are almost ready for harvesting. Plants such as honeysuckle, delphiniums and clematis, that show signs of yellowing leaves and blemishes, will also benefit from this treatment.

# 57

Leaves should never be burnt, unless they are diseased. Instead, use them to make leaf mould, a very useful material in any garden. Place the leaves in black plastic bin liners, and pack down. When full, tie the tops of the bags, pierce some holes with a garden fork, to allow excess moisture to escape, then store in a spare corner for two years or so. Neighbours with deciduous trees may be pleased to let you assist in clearing up their gardens, in return for providing a useful source of leaves! It stops them from polluting the atmosphere with a smoky bonfire, too!

# 58

For colour and foliage in the winter, there are some plants that are usually seen at their best when there is not much else on view. Among these are the Firethorn Pyracantha, Cotoneaster (variety Cornubia), and Holly Ilex. Remember, only the female Holly carries berries so there should be a male plant close at hand. The Dogwoods Cornus alba sibirica, with brilliant red stems, and Cornus sanquinea, with orange-red shoots, both add impressive colour to an otherwise drab winter garden. Both need hard pruning every other spring. For a splash of white or, sometimes, pink berries, the Rowan tree Sorbus hupehensis will eventually grow to around 8-10 metres, but also gives autumn colour; when young, its leaves have a distinctly blueish cast.

# 59

November is considered to be a good month to plant new, or move existing, trees and shrubs, to a new position in the garden. This gives them time to establish themselves before the harshness of winter sets in. Avoid planting too deeply. With container-grown trees and shrubs, plant about 10mm (½ inch) deeper than the pot surface: with bare root trees, plant as deep as the soil mark on the stem which shows the previous planting depth. Firm in well, using the heel of your boot to ensure that there are no soil voids around the roots that can lead to rotting or the tree rocking in the wind. A stake may be necessary; support the tree with a proper tree-tie or, alternatively, use discarded nylon tights.

# 60

Before planting any type of plant, water well while still in their containers, preferably a few hours beforehand. Never plant a dry plant! Also, ensure that the soil is moist before planting. Consider the use of a mulch around the plant to conserve moisture, and prevent weed growth; this mulch can be well-rotted compost, bark chips, or gravel, depending on the site, and availability. Water well after planting, and regularly thereafter, especially in warm, dry weather. Remember that plants in hanging baskets and terracotta containers will tend to dry out more quickly than those in the garden soil; regular watering is essential, as is feeding with a good, liquid plant food, to prolong flowering.

# 61

Frequent mowing encourages a dense growth of grass, and also keeps weeds down. During the growing season, weekly mowing is beneficial but don't cut it too short; regular cutting is less tiring than leaving it for a longer period, and can be beneficial in terms of the more gentle exercise involved, rather than the otherwise sheer hard work. Do not cut the lawn when the grass is slow growing, or in periods of hot, dry weather. Half an inch (around 12mm) is a reasonable length for grass on a flat lawn, and 1 inch (25mm) for uneven lawns or, where heavier traffic occurs.

# 62

Compost-accelerator products can be purchased that will assist in the composting but these are unnecessary, provided the conditions in the bin are satisfactory. Don't allow the compost to get too moist; add more drainage material, if necessary. Ensure that warmth is maintained for as long in the year as possible. After the first season, take all of the usable compost out of the bin or heap, for use in the garden, then turn over any non-composted material with a garden fork, to ensure good aeration, and return it to the bin. Take care not to harm or disturb any hibernating wildlife.

# 63

When the grass is growing strongly in the summer, rake once a month to remove thatch and moss that will leave brown patches if left unchallenged. In the spring, a top dressing of horticultural sand will promote growth, help to reduce the thatch, and also improve the soil structure. The occasional treatment with a combined lawn feed and weedkiller may be necessary but, on a lawn in good condition, no fertiliser is required other than mowing with the grass box removed now and then, to allow grass clippings to fertilise the lawn. Do not leave the box off if any lawn weeds have set seed.

# 64

Apart from the better-known varieties, such as the daffodil, narcissus, crocus, snowdrop, and hyacinth, there are other bulbs that can be grown both in the garden and in tubs and containers. Anemones, with their open saucer-shaped flowers, are available in many colours including pink, blue, purple, red and white. Fritillarias (varieties melegris and melegris albus) prefer a well-drained soil, and will produce drooping, bell-shaped flowers in white, pink, and purple. The Helleborus family has a number of varieties that bear flowers from late winter to early spring, in colours from white, through cream, to pink and purple; there is also a green variety Helleborus viridis.

# 65

Many a featureless garden can be enhanced by the addition of a rockery. While a bank or steep slope is ideal, an otherwise flat space can be transformed with the addition of a heap of topsoil, and some carefully selected rocks or large, flat stones. These stones should be embedded with their best face showing, and slope inwards towards the planting pockets to maximise the effect of rainfall or manual watering. The choice of soil is important, as some rockery or alpine plants, especially Gentian and Lithodora, will not tolerate alkaline conditions; the latter is an excellent, blue-flowered ground cover, but prefers a well-drained, sunny site.

# 66

Choose rockery plants carefully; a mix of individual alpine plants can look good, but take care not to let them be overshadowed by more vigorous varieties. After planting, water the new plants well, then cover the soil around them with coarse grit, or small shingle or gravel. This addition will both assist in drainage, and help to keep the roots cool; it can also improve the visual impact of the rockery, and will conserve moisture in warm weather. During dry weather, remember to water regularly. In spring, a liquid feed will be beneficial; rockeries need feeding, as do other parts of the garden.

# 67

Any garden can be made attractive to the more beneficial forms of wildlife. Some species that were once common in the garden are under threat, and in decline: try to encourage these forms of wildlife into the garden. If you provide food, shelter, and a source of water, it will encourage these gardener's assistants, and you will reap the rewards of better pollination of plants and natural pest control, and also derive pleasure from watching some of these creatures at work. To attract butterflies, plant single varieties of flowers, not hybrids. Single varieties are known to be more attractive to some species, as they tend to produce more pollen and nectar than the hybrid derivatives.

# 68

Birds, with a few notable exceptions, are beneficial visitors to the garden. The blackbird and the thrush are avid consumers of slugs, snails and worms, while the blue-tit thrives on aphids. Maintain the presence of these creatures in the garden by providing them with food during the harsher months of winter. A bird table, hanging feeder, and some scattered birdseed, will encourage most types of bird to the garden but, remember, you may not always attract the good guys – hungry birds of all over-wintering species will be attracted to your garden, including pigeons and gulls.

# 69

Apart from birds, hedgehogs and toads will help to keep the slug population under control. These creatures usually work the night shift, while the birds are resting after their daytime efforts. Try to encourage them by not using chemical treatments on the lawn, or on cultivated areas but, instead, use 'animal-safe' biological treatments. Strong lighting can deter some of these nocturnal visitors from entering your garden, so don't leave outside lights on, unless really necessary. Remember that the hedgehog may decide to spend its winter hibernation period in your compost heap or bonfire – check before using!

# 70

When planning a patio, consider the time of day during which it will be most used. Take note of where the sun will be at a given time of day, and plan accordingly. Bear in mind that some plants need more light, while others prefer shade. Depending on the size and aspect of the garden, the more fortunate gardener may have the best of both worlds and be able to grow both sun-loving and shade-loving plants. For the smaller or less sunny garden, the patio is still a viable site for plants, even though it may be brightly lit for only part of the day. Growing plants in wheeled planters, or a wheelbarrow, may provide a flexible solution to a sun or shade problem.

# 71

Badly damaged and weed-infested lawns are best taken up, the weeds and their roots removed, and the lawn relaid, either by seeding or re-turfing. If re-laying is necessary, take the opportunity to change the layout of the lawn, or even its position in the garden. Avoid areas beneath trees, or close to hedgerows or conifers, as all these will compete with the grass for moisture, and their shade will affect its growth. Lay the new lawn in late summer or early autumn, while the soil is still fairly warm, and water frequently.

# 72

Patio gardening can be either 'temporary' or 'permanent'; using bedding plants in the border of the patio, or in containers, can ensure a good display of colour. Temporary summer bedding plants of Geranium or Busy Lizzie, that last until early autumn, can be followed by Pansies and Forget-Me-Nots for the winter and spring. With careful selection of plant types and varieties, year-round colour is possible on almost any patio. Bulbs are also a popular choice for the patio, for a spring display of Crocus, Daffodil, and Tulip, while salad vegetables can add summer interest, as well as being useful in the kitchen.

# 73

Plants of a more permanent nature can be grown in containers on the patio. Low growing plants and shrubs can thrive in a place where they can be easily tended, and visible from the house. Perennials such as the Hostas, slow-growing Conifers and Roses, and even Box hedging can be grown successfully. Climbing plants can thrive on the patio, as can dwarf varieties of fruit trees, although these may require some form of support. Grown against a wall, or in containers, these climbers can cover unsightly walls or fencing, in addition to being attractive in their own right.

# 74

Containers should be as large as possible, to ensure good rooting. Good drainage is also important, so place some large terracotta pot pieces at the bottom, after first ensuring that the drain hole is clear. It is recommended that the container is placed on some brick or block supports, to raise it clear of the ground, and promote drainage. The use of a good potting compost is essential, as is regular feeding during the growing season. Frequent watering is necessary; remember that terracotta pots, although aesthetically pleasing, are naturally porous, and may dry out the compost more quickly than metal or plastic alternatives.

# 75

Turn containers frequently, at least once a week, to promote even growth and prevent them from becoming lopsided. This activity provides an opportunity to examine the plants for pests or weather damage, and any weeding that may be necessary; yes, weeds grow in containers, too! During the cropping season for salad vegetables and fruits, turning the pots will assist in ripening the produce – do not be tempted by the 'eat one as soon as it ripens' situation, if you hope to have a bumper crop; however, if you've earned it, take your reward, with the knowledge and satisfaction of having grown it yourself.

# 76

The types of tools needed in the garden will vary, depending on the size and design of your plot. A good tip is to buy only the best tools you can afford, those made from stainless steel are a good choice as they will last longer and be stronger, weight for weight, than those made from plain steel. The stainless tools are also easier to clean and, as the name implies, will not rust. This gives the additional benefit of making them easier to use; a stainless spade or fork will generally stay sharper, and cut through soil more readily, thus reducing the effort required.

# 77

Many gardeners make the mistake of buying the wrong tools for the job, and sometimes purchase more tools than are necessary. Choose tools that are of a size and weight that are comfortable to use. Stating the obvious, a tool that is comfortable for a tall, strong person may not be suitable for those of a shorter, or less powerful build. If the garden design features mainly small beds or borders, there is no need for the larger, powered tools and cultivator machines, whereas these will come into their own, and justify their cost, in the larger plot or allotment.

# 78

Before carrying out any work in the garden, ensure that you are dressed for the occasion. Good stout gardening boots, while not particularly fashionable, are the order of the day for most jobs; these can save injury to the feet, as well as providing a firm means of applying power to a spade or fork. Likewise, hand protection is necessary for most jobs in order to prevent injury, and reduce the likelihood of blisters to the hands. They also prevent the hands from becoming heavily soiled, and reduce the possibility of skin contact with chemicals, etc.

# 79

When using chemicals (if you must), always observe the precautions given on the container. Pay particular notice to advice regarding eye protection, prevention of over-spray, and the effects of wind. Most products should be applied when it is less breezy, just around sunset is ideal, to avoid affecting birds and other daytime visitors to your garden. Do not breathe in the fumes given off from any garden treatments, and keep children and pets away from the area. Dispose of any residue in a safe manner, and always wash out equipment after use. It is good practice to keep items specifically for the purpose; do not use the garden watering can!

# 80

As a minimum, a spade, fork, rake, and hoe, plus the essential watering can, will be necessary; these can be added to later, a wheelbarrow being one of the more useful items. If seed beds are being prepared, a garden sieve will come in handy when preparing the soil for smaller plants and seedlings. Many useful items can be obtained almost free of charge, by using cast-off household items to advantage; polythene food containers can be cut down into strips and used as plant labels, in conjunction with a permanent marker pen, or used to indicate the ends of rows when planting seeds.

# 81

For smaller tasks, a set of basic hand tools will prove invaluable. A trowel, hand fork, and a comfortable kneeler, will make the task much easier. A weed prong is useful for lifting weeds without breaking the root. Any broken weed root will almost certainly result in a new growth, so try to remove it completely. Pruning shears will assist in keeping shrubs and fruit trees under control, so buy the best you can afford. Any garden centre or nursery will advise on the selection of this important tool.

# 82

Consider the use of a tool belt when carrying out work requiring smaller tools. There is nothing more frustrating than to kneel down to attend to a plant, only to discover that you have left the tool just out of reach or worse, when changing position, to receive a painful reminder that you have knelt or sat upon the offending item. For larger tasks, collect all of the tools you think you will need for the job, and transport them in the wheelbarrow to the workplace. Keep all tools not actually in use well away from the area being worked on; stepping on the tines of a rake may be funny in a cartoon but, in reality, could result in a nasty injury.

# 83

When choosing a lawn mower, consider what type of lawn you are hoping to achieve, and get the correct machine for the job. While you may fancy the idea, funds permitting, of riding around your grassed area on a tractor mower, the finished result is unlikely to resemble a bowling green or croquet lawn. Generally, mowers with rotary blades will not produce as good a result as a cylinder mower. The cylinder mower will produce a much finer finish, with the proviso that the lawn surface must be fairly flat, to avoid 'scuffing' when the cut is set low.

# 84

A mower with a grass collector box will help to keep the grassed area looking tidy, as well as providing a labour-saving means of collecting the clippings that can be used as mulch, or on the compost heap. Some types of mower, especially those that use the 'hover' principle, are especially suitable for use on uneven ground, or steep slopes and banks: some of these actually cut so finely that they effectively mulch the lawn, the down-side being that there is little or no compostable material remaining. Keep the mower in good condition; sharp blades will make grass-cutting a much easier task, and result in a better finish.

# Also available:

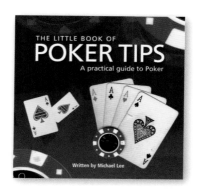

**The pictures in this book were provided courtesy of**

GETTY IMAGES
www.gettyimages.com

SHUTTERSTOCK IMAGES
www.shutterstock.com

Design and artwork by David Wildish

Image research by Ellie Charleston

Creative Director: Kevin Gardner

Published by Green Umbrella Publishing

Publishers: Jules Gammond, Vanessa Gardner

Written by David Curnock